The Hidden World of
Garbage

Multi-Digit Numbers

Katie McKissick

Consultants

Michele Ogden, Ed.D
Principal
Irvine Unified School District

Colleen Pollitt, M.A.Ed.
Math Support Teacher
Howard County Public Schools

Publishing Credits

Rachelle Cracchiolo, M.S.Ed., *Publisher*
Conni Medina, M.A.Ed., *Managing Editor*
Dona Herweck Rice, *Series Developer*
Emily R. Smith, M.A.Ed., *Series Developer*
Diana Kenney, M.A.Ed., NBCT, *Content Director*
Stacy Monsman, M.A., *Editor*
Kevin Panter, *Graphic Designer*

Image Credits: pp. 6–7 Jerry Cooke/The LIFE Images Collection/Getty Images; pp. 14–15 benedek/Getty Images; p. 19 (top) Brent Lewin/Bloomberg via Getty Images, (bottom) James King-Holmes/Science Source; p. 21 (top) Joel Page/Portland Press Herald via Getty Images; p. 23 (top) Martin Bond/Science Source; p. 27 (bottom) Realimage/Alamy Stock Photo; all other images from iStock and/or Shutterstock.

Library of Congress Cataloging-in-Publication Data

Names: McKissick, Katie, author.
Title: The hidden world of garbage / Katie McKissick.
Description: Huntington Beach, CA : Teacher Created Materials, [2018] | Includes index.
Identifiers: LCCN 2017011805 (print) | LCCN 2017014707 (ebook) | ISBN 9781480759282 (eBook) | ISBN 9781425855468 (pbk.)
Subjects: LCSH: Refuse and refuse disposal--Juvenile literature. | Refuse and refuse disposal--Statistics--Juvenile literature.
Classification: LCC TD792 (ebook) | LCC TD792 .M37 2018 (print) | DDC 628.4/45--dc23
LC record available at https://lccn.loc.gov/2017011805

Teacher Created Materials

5301 Oceanus Drive
Huntington Beach, CA 92649-1030
http://www.tcmpub.com

ISBN 978-1-4258-5546-8

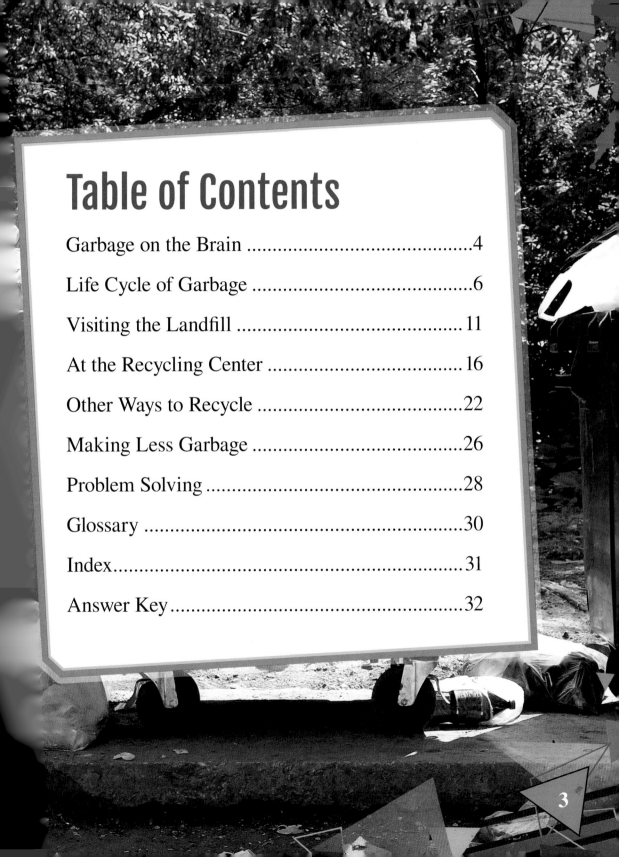

Table of Contents

Garbage on the Brain

It's stinky. It's smelly. Chances are, you've probably never thought much about it. It's garbage. Can you remember the last thing you threw away? Was it an apple core? Was it a napkin? Was it something that could be **recycled**? People might not spend hours each day thinking about trash. But, what and how things are thrown away are important.

How much garbage do people make in a day, a week, or even a year? How much does a whole city, or even the whole world, throw away? The amount of garbage must be immense! What happens to it? Why doesn't garbage fill most streets? For something people don't spend a lot of time thinking about, there sure are a lot of questions about garbage!

DO NOT PARK
NO HAZARDOUS
WASTES ACCEPTED

CAUTION NOTICE
DO NOT PLAY IN
OR ON
THIS CONTAINER

CONTAINER
MUST BE PLACED
ON HARD LEVEL
SURFACE AND LOADED
UNIFORMLY

CAUTION

DO NOT CLIMB
ON OR ENTER
THIS CONTAINER

TRASH

5

Life Cycle of Garbage

It might not seem like it, but garbage can be a big deal—a very big deal. On average, one person makes about 4 pounds (2 kilograms) of garbage per day. That totals 1,460 lbs. (662 kg) each year. That's about how much a cow weighs!

All of that garbage needs to go somewhere. Otherwise, the streets would be full of stale bread, dirty diapers, and brown apple cores. That's where garbage collectors come in. They collect garbage with trucks. Garbage trucks have been around since the 1800s. But, how they look has changed quite a bit. They started as open-air carts hauled by horses. As carts rolled down the roads, garbage often flew out of the cart and back into the street! It wasn't until the 1920s that closed trucks made their way into common use.

On average, a person makes 122 pounds of trash in one month. How is the value of the 2 in the tens place different from the value of the 2 in the ones place? Use your understanding of place value to explain your reasoning.

Garbage collectors haul away trash using a horse-drawn garbage wagon in 1946.

Garbage trucks of today are huge, powerful machines. One truck can haul garbage from more than 800 houses. And each truck can hold more than 10 tons (9,072 kg) of garbage! Once collected, the trash is taken to a transfer station.

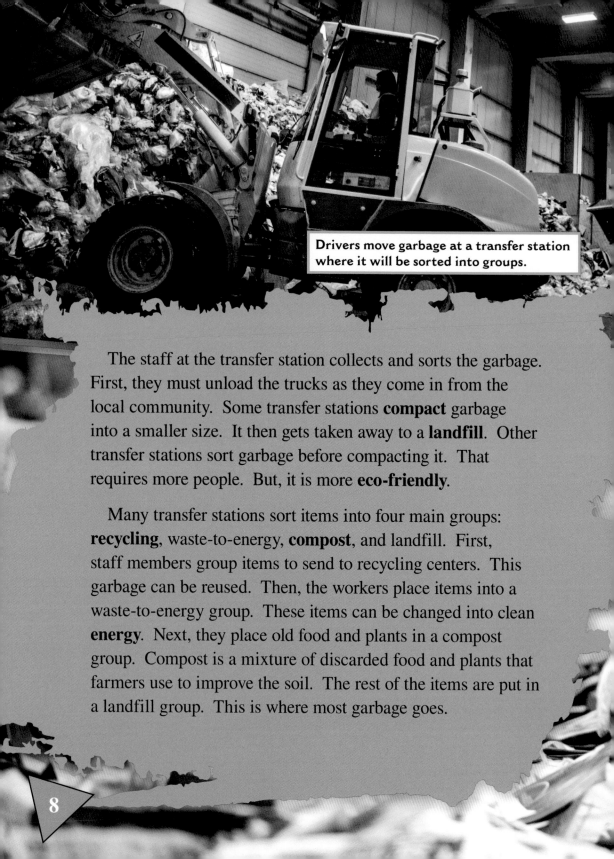

Drivers move garbage at a transfer station where it will be sorted into groups.

The staff at the transfer station collects and sorts the garbage. First, they must unload the trucks as they come in from the local community. Some transfer stations **compact** garbage into a smaller size. It then gets taken away to a **landfill**. Other transfer stations sort garbage before compacting it. That requires more people. But, it is more **eco-friendly**.

Many transfer stations sort items into four main groups: **recycling**, waste-to-energy, **compost**, and landfill. First, staff members group items to send to recycling centers. This garbage can be reused. Then, the workers place items into a waste-to-energy group. These items can be changed into clean **energy**. Next, they place old food and plants in a compost group. Compost is a mixture of discarded food and plants that farmers use to improve the soil. The rest of the items are put in a landfill group. This is where most garbage goes.

A man sorts paper products at a recycling center.

A compactor flattens garbage in a landfill.

Visiting the Landfill

Over half of the garbage that gets picked up will head to a landfill. But, there is much more to a landfill than the name suggests. Gone are the days when garbage trucks would simply drop trash into a large hole and cover it with dirt. Now, landfills are built into the ground. Garbage is taken to specific areas. There may be different areas each day. A **compactor** drives over the new garbage until it is flat. Then, workers cover it with dirt. This helps keep odors from escaping.

Once garbage is packed underground, it begins to **decay**. During this process, the decayed garbage releases **methane** gas. In some places, methane is collected and used to make electricity. Sometimes, garbage decays quickly. Plants, food, and paper all decay within a few months. Other trash takes much longer. It can take up to 1,000 years for a single plastic bottle to break down. That is why it is best to recycle plastic. Still, many recyclables end up in landfills.

LET'S EXPLORE MATH

Imagine that the methane gas from one landfill can be converted into electricity to power 2,385 homes per year. Another landfill produces enough methane gas to power 2,435 homes per year.

1. How can place value be used to compare these numbers? Explain your thinking.

2. Write a comparison statement with the numbers using >, <, or =.

What types of garbage might people find at a landfill? About one-third of the waste is packaging material. Most of this consists of **corrugated** cardboard. Americans discard more than 29 million tons (26 billion kg) of cardboard each year. Imagine how much corrugated cardboard is thrown away in the entire world!

Most corrugated cardboard that is thrown away is recycled. Nine out of 10 pieces to be exact! But even the 1 out of 10 pieces that aren't recycled add up to millions of tons of waste. New trees have to be cut down to make cardboard for the next year. In fact, over 15 million trees are cut down each year to make cardboard. And, that's just in the United States. If people all over the world stopped recycling, trees would be chopped down way too quickly to replace.

Suppose a garbage truck company collects 25,376 pounds of cardboard.

1. Draw a number line and plot 25,376. Between which two thousands does 25,376 fall?

2. Use your number line to round 25,376 to the nearest thousand.

Trucks transport plastic and cardboard to a recycling center.

The Bottle House in Canada is made of 500,000 glass bottles.

14

It is not possible to recycle some forms of waste. Paint cans, certain metals, paper containers with plastic liners, and some types of plastic are examples. But, that does not mean these items have to go straight to landfills.

Some people get creative with **nonrecyclables**. Sometimes, people reuse common items. They may make art out of pieces of broken glass or wallets out of plastic folders. Soup cans may be made into jewelry. Plastic cups may be used as pencil cases. And soda bottles may be used to grow plants.

Some people even take their reusing a step further. They turn huge tires into planters. They use milk jugs to make storage for school supplies. A house in Canada was even built with glass bottles!

At the Recycling Center

There are many creative ways to reuse things. But, what happens when trash is recycled? Paper, plastic, and glass each go through a special process to turn into something new.

Precious Paper

Every year, each American recycles about 275 lbs. (125 kg) of paper. But there is still a lot of paper that ends up in landfills. Imagine if every newspaper printed in the United States were recycled. The world could save about 250 million trees per year! Now, add that to all the mail, sticky notes, and other scraps of paper people use in a year. Clearly, recycling paper can have a big impact on the environment!

The types of products made from recycled paper are based on how the paper is made. Paper is made with **fibers** taken from trees. As it is recycled, the fibers shorten. Paper with short fibers gets made into tissue or toilet paper. Paper with long fibers gets made into printing paper.

When paper is recycled, it is first chopped into small pieces. Then, it's mixed with water. It turns into a mush. This sludge is spread out and dried to make new paper. It can be made into books, plates, napkins, and more.

A machine mixes bits of paper and water to turn it into new paper.

Mounds of paper are ready for recycling.

Popular Plastic

The average person uses about 125 pieces of plastic each week. In a year, that could add up to 6,500 pieces. When all of the people in the world are considered, that much plastic could circle Earth four times!

This doesn't mean that all hope is lost for a cleaner planet. People can use less plastic and save money. One way is by drinking water from reusable bottles. It costs about 700 times more to buy bottled water than it does to drink water out of the tap. That means that if a person buys a $1 bottle of water each day for a year, they would spend $365. If they were to fill a reusable bottle with tap water each day for a year, they would only spend $0.52!

Still, there might be times when using a plastic water bottle is unavoidable. In those cases, it's important to recycle. Recycling bottles costs less than making new ones. And, recycling plastic helps save animals. Over a million animals are killed each year by plastic that has not been recycled. So, it is best for everyone when people recycle plastic.

plastic containers

LET'S EXPLORE MATH

It is estimated that one person uses 125 pieces of plastic each week. Write 125 at least three different ways.

Plastic bottles pass through a sorting machine at a recycling center.

So what happens when plastic is recycled? Recycling centers first crush the plastic. The crushed plastic is cleaned and sorted. The sorting is based on the types of products the plastic will be turned into. Then, it is ground into flakes and washed and sorted again. Finally, it's melted and turned into new things. It can be made into new bottles, pipes, chairs, and even clothes!

plastic flakes

A factory worker handles hot bottles formed from recycled glass.

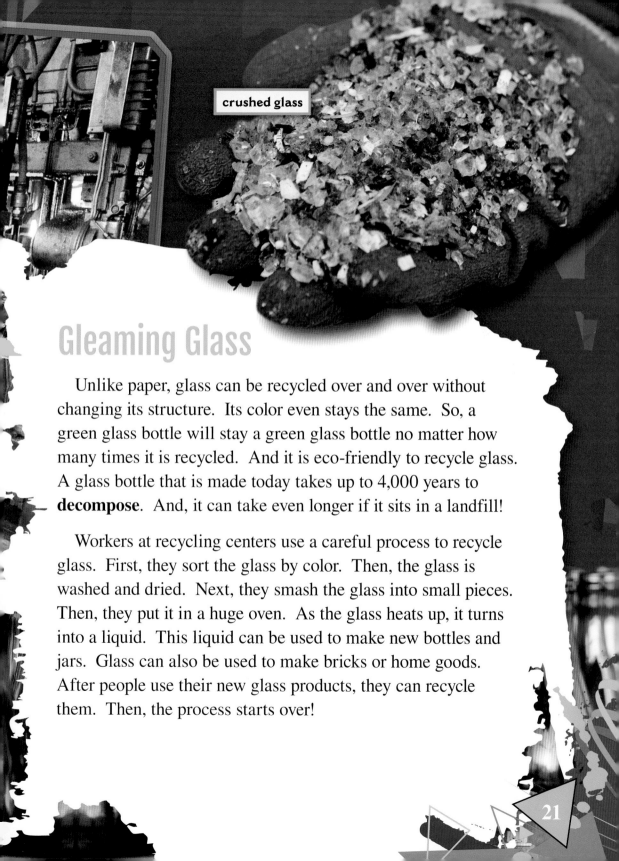

crushed glass

Gleaming Glass

Unlike paper, glass can be recycled over and over without changing its structure. Its color even stays the same. So, a green glass bottle will stay a green glass bottle no matter how many times it is recycled. And it is eco-friendly to recycle glass. A glass bottle that is made today takes up to 4,000 years to **decompose**. And, it can take even longer if it sits in a landfill!

Workers at recycling centers use a careful process to recycle glass. First, they sort the glass by color. Then, the glass is washed and dried. Next, they smash the glass into small pieces. Then, they put it in a huge oven. As the glass heats up, it turns into a liquid. This liquid can be used to make new bottles and jars. Glass can also be used to make bricks or home goods. After people use their new glass products, they can recycle them. Then, the process starts over!

Other Ways to Recycle

People are always looking for new ways to reduce garbage. Some people think burning trash is the answer. Other people love composting.

Waste-to-Energy Plants

Waste-to-energy plants are a fairly new idea in the United States. In fact, there are only about 70 in the whole country. On one side of the debate are people who are concerned about air, water, and soil pollution. On the other side of the debate are people who love the energy it creates. Each year, burned trash is used to power over a million homes! So, how does it work?

waste-to-energy plant

Factory workers at a waste-to-energy plant sort the garbage they receive in a month. The staff counts 2,400 plastic water bottles. There are 10 times as many aluminum cans. How can you find the number of aluminum cans? Explain your reasoning.

A waste-to-energy plant worker shovels trash pellets that will be burned.

First, garbage is brought to the plants. The staff checks it to make sure that it can be used. About 85 out of every 100 things thrown away can be burned. So, most of the things they sort are fit for use. After that, the garbage is taken to a pit. A huge crane picks up trash from the pit and loads it into a **combustion** chamber. As the garbage burns, water turns into steam. This steam can be turned into electricity. For every 2,000 lbs. (907 kg) of garbage burned at a plant, enough energy is formed to power 16 homes.

compost

Composting

Another way people can reduce waste is by putting used food items back into the soil instead of throwing them away. Almost two-thirds of household waste can be **composted**. Compost is a mixture of leaves, plants, and food. These things can be put in the soil. As they decay, they help new plants and food grow.

Composting is a simple process. As food and plants are added to the pile, they begin to decompose. Then, the compost becomes a **fertilizer** that helps to improve the quality of the soil. The new fertilizer can be spread across farms and gardens. New plants and food items can grow from the **nutrient**-rich soil.

Some communities and schools have started composting programs. An average school creates over 3,000 lbs. (1,300 kg) of food waste each year. Most of it comes from the lunchroom. Instead of just throwing away banana peels and apple cores after lunch, students put them into compost piles. Schools that compost save money by not having as much garbage. And, the compost can be used in school gardens. As fruits and vegetables grow, students and teachers can grab snacks throughout the day. The uneaten remains can be put back into the compost pile!

Making Less Garbage

People make garbage at a stunning rate. For many years, people thought burying it was the best way to go. In recent years, people have recycled more garbage than ever before. And each year, this amount continues to rise. But there is still a long way to go. Most of the garbage that is thrown away still goes straight to landfills.

There are other options, though. Reusing water bottles and sorting recyclables are easy and cost-effective ways to help. Making compost piles is another way to help. With so many options available, people can choose the one that makes the most sense for them. If people all pitch in before they pitch it out, they can make a lasting impact for years to come.

MADE OF
100%
RECYCLED
PAPER

Plastic water bottles can be reused to grow vegetables.

I used to be a plastic bottle

⚙️ Problem Solving

Jillian wants to start a compost pile at her school. She asks her classmates to put their old food into a special container outside the cafeteria. The students have decided to use the compost pile to grow a vegetable garden. That way, they can all have healthy snacks at school. And they might even be able to take some food home to their families. To see how large of a vegetable garden they can make, Jillian has been keeping track of all of the food items put in the compost pile in the first month. Use Jillian's list to answer the questions.

List of Food Items

- 29 watermelon rinds
- 157 carrot tops
- 238 banana peels
- 1,213 apple cores

1. Write the number of carrot tops in word form and expanded form.

2. How is the value of the 3 in 238 banana peels different from the value of the 3 in 1,213 apple cores?

3. About how many of each food item has Jillian composted so far? Draw a number line and plot each number. Then, round each number to its greatest place value.

4. Use your number line to compare the number of carrot tops with the number of banana peels. Write a comparison statement with the numbers using >, <, or =. Explain your thinking.

5. Suppose Jillian composts two thousand, four hundred seven slices of moldy bread. Write this number in at least three different ways.

FOR COMPOSTING

Glossary

combustion—a chemical reaction that produces heat

compact—to press something together so that it takes up less space

compactor—a machine that presses garbage to reduce its size

compost—a decayed mixture of plants and food that is reused as soil

composted—the process by which decayed plants and food are turned into soil

corrugated—a type of cardboard with many folds

decay—to rot or spoil

decompose—to break something down into its individual parts

eco-friendly—not harmful to the environment

energy—power that can be used to do something

fertilizer—nutrients that are added to soil from decomposing plants or animals

fibers—thin threads

landfill—an area where garbage is buried

methane—a gas that is released during decomposition

nonrecyclables—items that cannot be processed or treated for further use

nutrient—a substance that living things need to grow

recycled—the process of making a material into something new

recycling—the act of reusing a material or making it into something new

Index

Answer Key

Let's Explore Math

page 7:

The value of the 2 in the tens place is 10 times greater than the value of the 2 in the ones place. 2 tens (20) is 10 times greater than 2 ones (2).

page 11:

1. Since the values of the thousands places are the same in both numbers, compare the values of the hundreds places. 2,385 has 3 hundreds and 2,435 has 4 hundreds.

2. 2,385 < 2,435 or 2,435 > 2,385

page 13:

1. Number lines should show 25,376 between 25,000 and 26,000, but closer to 25,000; between 25,000 and 26,000

2. 25,000

page 19:

one hundred twenty-five;
100 + 20 + 5;
1 hundred, 2 tens, 5 ones;
12 tens and 5 ones

page 23:

24,000 aluminum cans; 20,000 is 10 times greater than 2,000, and 4,000 is 10 times greater than 400

Problem Solving

1. One hundred fifty-seven; 100 + 50 + 7

2. The value of 3 in 238 is 10 times greater than the value of 3 in 1,213. 3 tens (30) is 10 times greater than 3 ones (3).

3. Watermelon rinds: 30; carrot tops: 200; banana peels: 200; apple cores: 1,000; Number lines should show each exact number plotted near the estimates.

4. 157 < 238 or 238 > 157; 100 is less than 200 or 200 is greater than 100

5. Answers will vary, but may include: 2,407; 2,000 + 400 + 7; 2 thousands, 4 hundreds, 7 ones; 24 hundreds and 7 ones